# YOUR KNOWLEDGE HAS VALUE

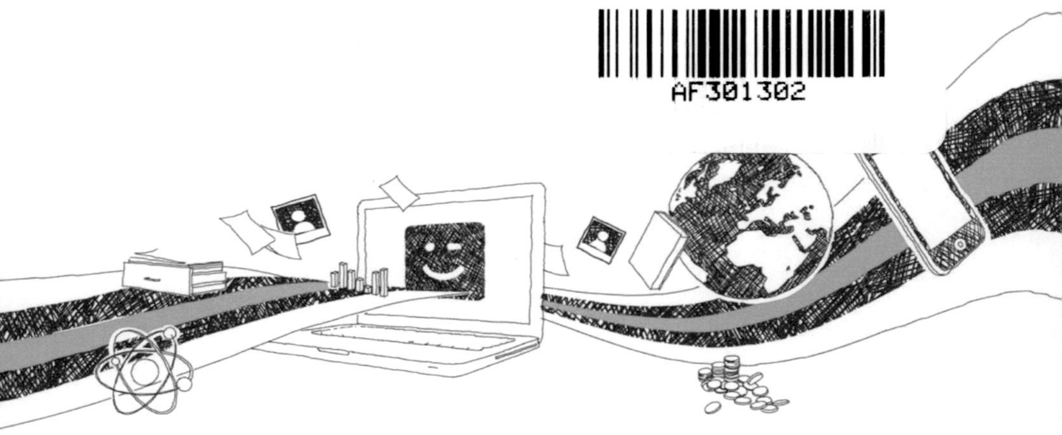

- We will publish your bachelor's and
  master's thesis, essays and papers

- Your own eBook and book -
  sold worldwide in all relevant shops

- Earn money with each sale

Upload your text at www.GRIN.com
and publish for free

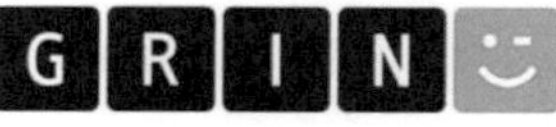

Sarah Doerfel

# How does the use of Gerhard Richter's blur technique in his cycle "October 18, 1977" change the effect of the paintings in comparison to the original source images?

GRIN Verlag

**Bibliografische Information der Deutschen Nationalbibliothek:**

Die Deutsche Bibliothek verzeichnet diese Publikation in der Deutschen National-bibliografie; detaillierte bibliografische Daten sind im Internet über http://dnb.d-nb.de/ abrufbar.



**Imprint:**

Copyright © 2011 GRIN Verlag GmbH
Druck und Bindung: Books on Demand GmbH, Norderstedt Germany
ISBN: 978-3-656-35524-3

**This book at GRIN:**

http://www.grin.com/en/e-book/208046/how-does-the-use-of-gerhard-richter-s-blur-technique-in-his-cycle-october

**Sarah Doerfel**
**Module: Perspectives in Photography**
**University of Westminster, London**
**2011**

*How does the use of Gerhard Richter's blur technique in his cycle "October 18, 1977"*
*change the effect of the paintings in comparison to the original source images?*

Gerhard Richter is one of the most successful contemporary artists. His work is known for being very diverse and having no specific style seems to be his style. His apparent lack of a clear commitment to a style, an opinion, or a political standpoint can also be found in his blur technique which he uses for his paintings from photographic originals: blurring the originally sharp images abstracts them. Richter's point of view seems to be hidden behind a thin but insurmountable curtain. The blur also keeps the viewer from seeing clear himself, from judging the situation, from taking on a standpoint. The painter has to confront this criticism of having no opinion especially with his political historical subjects, like the paintings "Onkel Rudi /Uncle Rudi" (1965) or "Tante Marianne/ Aunt Marianne" (1965), which show relatives of Richter in the context of Nazi Germany. Apart from these, especially the cycle "October 18, 1977" made onlookers search for the artist's opinion and intention, as these 15 paintings do not show a political subject represented on the basis of family photographs, like his earlier works. The cycle's source images are press and police photographs and it deals with the events around the Baader- Meinhof gang, a group of terrorists active in Germany in the 1970s. At the time Richter chose to paint this subject, the events had already passed for more than a decade, which seems like he wanted to say something about it that he felt was missing but essential to close this chapter of history. Viewers and critics are therefore looking for his statement in the painting but cannot find what they expect. The painter is criticized for picking a controversial subject, attracting attention to the issue, raising questions but refusing to offer an opinion and refuse an answer. The artist himself, though, says, that "the political topicality of my October paintings means almost nothing to me" (Richter, 1968, n.p.).

In the following essay I want to concentrate on the blur effect in Richter's cycle "October, 18 1977". I want to show how the blur changed the effect of the source photographs and that the artist's statement lies exactly there. When generally "blur" stands for obscuring the clear sight on a subject, this is arguable for the cycle: Through the blur, the viewer here much more gets the chance of a real encounter with these images. This essay will focus on the comparison of the effect of the original photographs and Richter's version, basing on the six paintings "Erhängte/ Hanged" (1988), "Erschossener 1/ Man Shot Down 1" (1988), "Erschossener 2/ Man Shot Down 2" (1988), and the three images "Tote/ Dead" (1988). I will not go into detail about the biographical context that shaped Richter's political and painterly approach.


The German RAF (Red Army Faction) terrorists Ulrike Meinhof, Andreas Baader, Gudrun Ensslin and others were arrested in 1972 and spent the last years of their lives in the German prison Stammheim near Stuttgart. In 1976 Meinhof committed suicide in her cell by hanging herself. On 18 October 1977 Baader, Ensslin and other RAF members decided to jointly follow their friend by committing suicide in their respective cells. Press and police photographers took images of their belongings, rooms and their bodies and the shocking pictures were published in German newspapers and magazines.

These press photographs do not commiserate what they depict, they are there for the simple fact of informing and documenting, of showing what the situation looked like. Looking at these images, we have the feeling of intruding in the prisoners' privacy, of taking part in the photographer's voyeuristic act. Susan Sontag explains on this topic: "But there is shame as well as shock in looking at the close-up of a real horror. Perhaps the only people with the right to look at images of suffering of this extreme order are those who could do something to alleviate it (…). The rest of us are voyeurs, whether or not we mean to be" (2003, p.37-38).

The press photographs ruthlessly show Meinhof's head and neck in very close up after she hanged herself (Fig. 6), Baader on the floor of his cell with open eyes and the gun next to his head in a puddle of blood (Fig. 1), and Ensslin hanging in front of an open window on an electric cable (Fig. 4). If another well known personality dies, we are usually not shown photographs displaying their bloody bodies, or deformed body parts. Such pictures would not be published because this seems to cross a border of respect for the dead. The display of a dead person in his disfigured state is still considered unethical, even in our times of often low borders of respect.

The photographer showing the dead in this undignified moment is exposing them. This exposition is officially tolerated because the terrorists have lost their right of respectable treatment; the exposition is justified by the terrorists' acts of cruelty, it becomes a form of publicly punishing them for what they have done. By looking at the images of the dead RAF members in newspapers or on TV, the viewer collaborates with the photographer in the voyeuristic act, takes part in this punishment and exposure by being the audience to whom the disfigured corpse is displayed. "People can't wait to see corpses. They crave sensations"

(Richter, 1989, p. 185) and feel less guilty about this act knowing the body they are looking at is of a terrorist than of somebody else.

For all these facts, the original press images of the death of the RAF terrorists are too direct and too inappropriate to be really accessible, they do not leave the possibility of sinking into them, of spending time with them and reflecting on them. Or as Robert Storr, curator of Richter's show "October 18, 1977" at the Museum of Modern Art, New York, puts it: "Physically restless as much as troubled by the confrontation with mortality we move on. In photographs we can see death with a nakedness no other medium affords. But photography does not allow us to contemplate death"(2000, p.103).

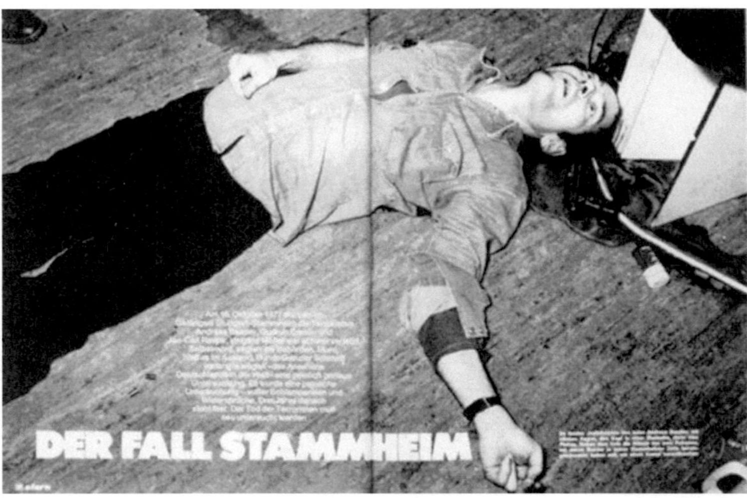


Der Stern, *Andreas Baader, dead* (1977)

Fig. 1

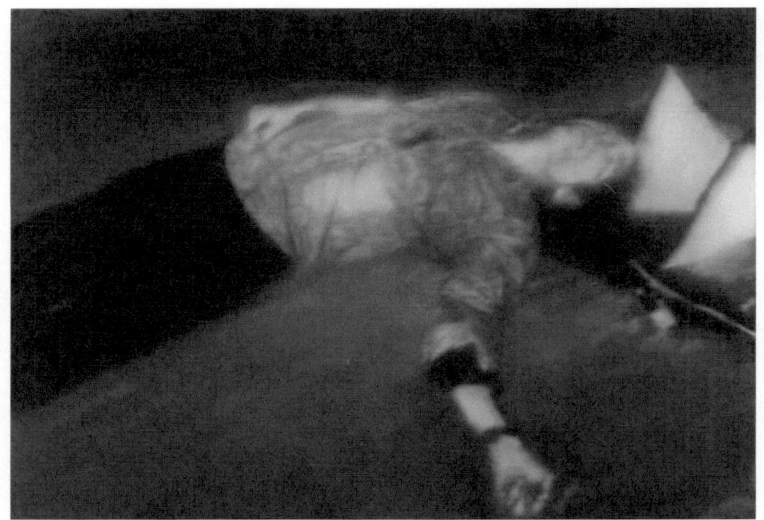

Gerhard Richter, *Man Shot Down 1* (1988)

Fig. 2

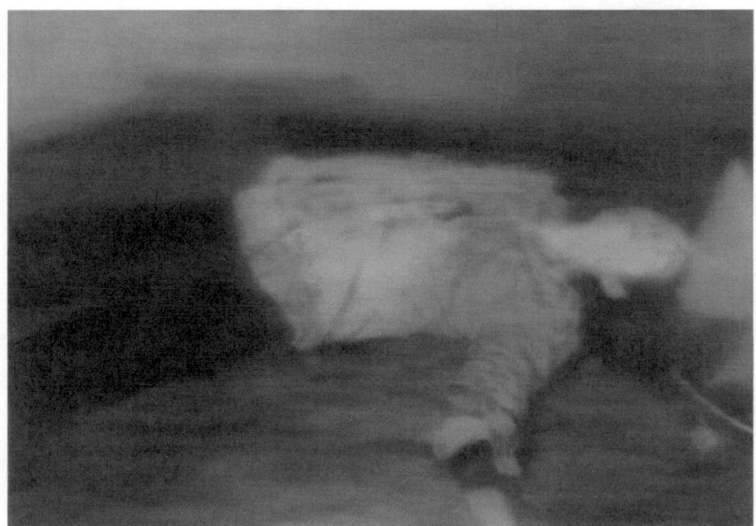

Gerhard Richter, *Man Shot Down 2* (1988)

Fig. 3

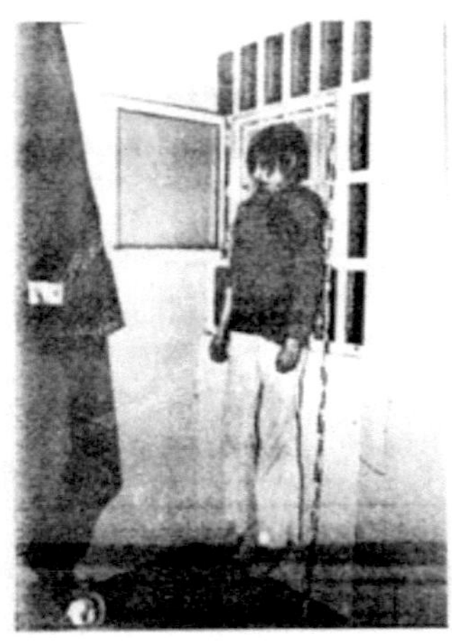

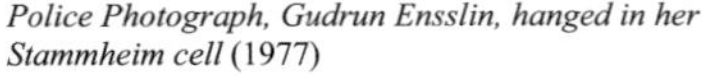

*Police Photograph, Gudrun Ensslin, hanged in her Stammheim cell* (1977)

Fig. 4

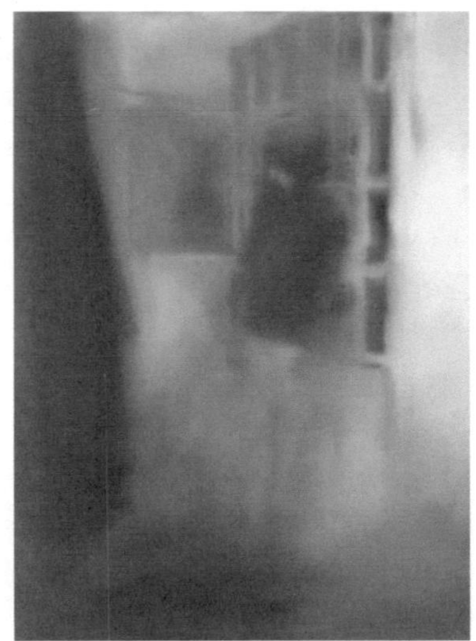

Gerhard Richter, *Hanged* (1988)

Fig. 5

Comparing this to Richter's paintings, "the artist's use of blurring serves to erase the graphic brutality of the photographs published in the media, and to minimalize the hint of voyeurism" (Elger, 2009, p.284). By painting these images, and by turning their directness into indirectness through the blur effect, Richter corrects the original images. They are put right through the blur because respect returns into the situation, with the new distance to the object. The blur enables us to experience the situation in a different way: It is a means of subsequently building in distance into the situation which helps us to confront the strong images at all. "The artist's subtle manipulations downplay all the sensational qualities the mass media exploited" (Storr, 2000, p. 106).Viewing Richter's paintings we do not have to feel like voyeurs anymore, we can bear the situation looking at the dead and confront our thoughts and feelings better than with the overwhelmingly direct originals. "The paintings were based on shocking images, rendered tolerable only through Richter's transformation" (Elger, 2009, p.300).

Apart from making the images more tolerable through the distance of blur, the same blurred quality is also what tortures the viewer. It also plays on our desire for intensity and sensation. The blur can even make us angry because we are not allowed to see more, only a teaser of what happened. We are left with the need of facts, details, left with our growing curiosity and desire to lift the layer of blur, to switch it off, looking at one painting after another only getting the same imprecision, the same anti matter-of-factness. The blur has the ability of "underlying the despair that seems evenly spread across [the paintings], there is anger" (Storr, 2000, p.96) in these images.

This culminates in the two images "Man Shot Down 1/ 2" (Fig. 2-3) and the three images "Dead": here Richter chose several versions he painted of the same original photograph to be part of his cycle. All of them are blurred – if the viewer tries to find additional details in the second or third painting, to make up for the blur, he will not find anything (Fig. 7-9). Looking at the repetition of a blurred theme without getting any further information can provoke, especially as the subject - death and violence - naturally arouses our desire to see more. The blur tries to tame this longing of the viewer, it patronizes him, as it decides for him what he is allowed to see or not. All this reflects the paralysed feeling of being imprisoned, of the RAF inmates, who were inferior to their enemy, the State. The blurred quality of the cycle tortures and paralyzes the viewer, mirroring a feeling of being captured, locked in, a feeling of swoon, of helplessness and weakness. The blur forces us to hold back our curiosity and we know it will not change, we will never find more details in these images, uncertainty is definite. "This blurring is therefore both subjective act and objective state at one and the same time" (Koch, 1992, p.37). We have to suppress our urge for clarity as viewers, as the terrorists were carrying their forbidden revolutionary ideas until the end, with growing anger. This rage finally culminated in their suicide, which stands to some extent for the failure of their ideals and their capitulation under the inner pressure. Richter says: "Deadly reality, inhuman reality. Our rebellion. Impotence. Failure. Death. – that is why I paint these pictures" (Richter, 1988, p.175). "This has to do with the everlasting human dilemma in general: to work for a revolution and fail" (Richter, 1989, p.194).

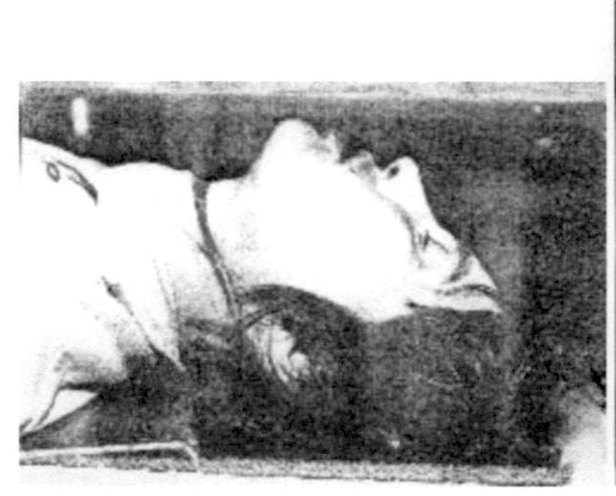
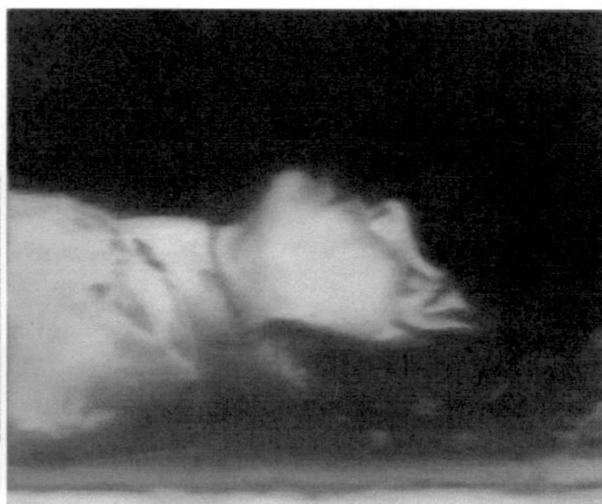

Der Stern, *Ulrike Meinhof, dead* (1976)       Gerhard Richter, *Dead* (1988)

Fig. 6                                          Fig. 7

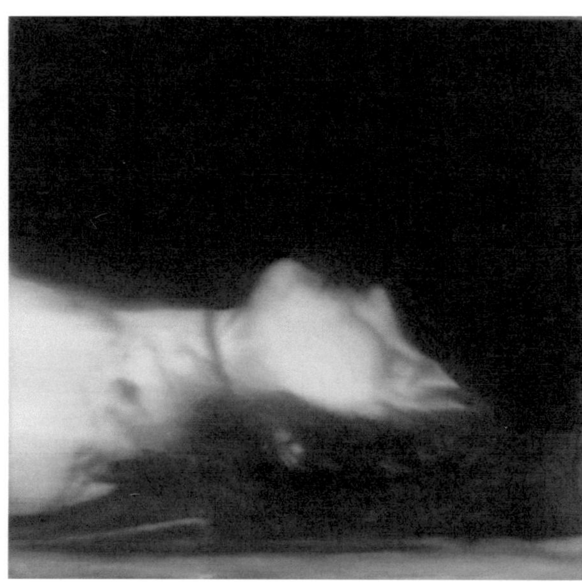

Gerhard Richter, *Dead* (1988)

Fig. 8

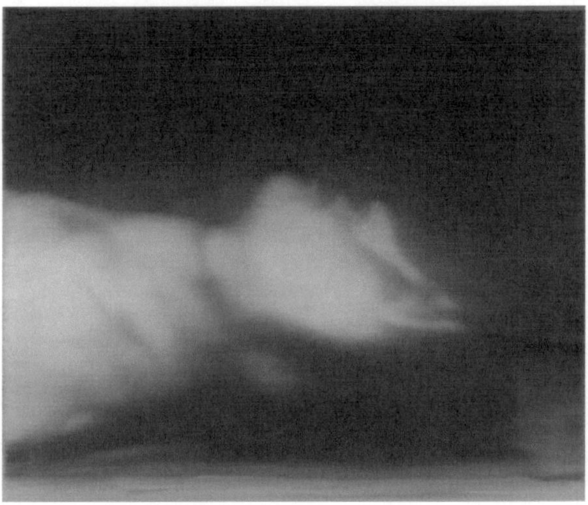

Gerhard Richter, *Dead* (1988)

Fig. 9

Another effect of the blur, and maybe its most important one, is that it abstracts what happened and so takes the subject to a general level: we are looking at humans in a tragic situation and not at the dangerous terrorists that finally found their deserved death, that the press images show us. The blur takes away the scandalous look of the originals and shows the situation in a very different light. "In *October 18, 1977* we are not looking at average, redundant death but an exemplary suffering" (Storr, 2000, p.111). The blurred paintings show the joint suicide as a last act of winning back self-determination - not as mad and irresponsible terrorists - but as humans who stand in with an immense will power for what they think. The artist says, he "was impressed by the terrorists' energy, their uncompromising determination and their absolute bravery" (Richter, 1988, p.173). To acknowledge these attributes, dignity had to return into the situation, which the blur effect made possible (Fig. 5). As Storr explains: "Those who take a less-than-full account of the human pain and sadness embedded in *October 18, 1977* in haste to integrate them into narrowly defined social or formal discourses do the work a disservice (…). Taken together, these are not "aesthetic" sentiments, or matters of opinion, they are empathetic responses to suffering, and Richter's work is frankly intended to stimulate similar responses in the viewer" (2000, p.133).

Through the blur, it becomes possible to see the situation, the same images, in a very different light. The images become a personal encounter that does not feel unethical anymore. The paintings allow us to be there, but in a new, respectful situation that is staged by Richter with the help of the blur. He explains: "It is impossible for me to interpret the pictures. That is: in the first place they are too emotional; they are, if possible, an expression of a speechless emotion. They are the almost forlorn attempt to give shape to feelings of compassion, grief and horror (as if the pictorial repetition of the events were a way of understanding those events, being able to live with them" (1988, p.174).

All in all, the cycle becomes a statement of a different kind than we would expect to get when being shown images of such a political content as the RAF. Richter manages by the use of the blur, to show human suffering in a sentimental and tragic way on the base of political images. The blur allows us to take a deeper look into the historic situation in a merely emotional way, it confronts us with the feelings of despair and anger of the prisoners, it shows their very human side by turning the images of the terrorists' suicides into an allegory of human suffering. Richter does not want to give his political opinion on the subject but show that there is another side to it: the very human side. This is where his intention lies and the blur is his means of delivering it. As Susan Sontag explains,"there is the satisfaction of being able to look at the image without flinching. There is the pleasure of flinching" (2003, p.37). When the strong press images can give the viewer the "pleasure of flinching", Richter's blur enables his paintings to satisfy the viewer because he does not have to flinch anymore, he can take his time looking at them.

**Bibliography**

Elger, D., (2009). *Gerhard Richter – A Life in Painting*. Chicago and London: The University of Chicago Press.

Koch, G., (1992). *The Richter-Scale of Blur – Gerhard Richter -  October Files*. Cambridge, Massachusetts: MIT Press.

Richter, G., (1968). *Arbeitsübersicht [Work Overview] - 14x14. Junge deutsche Künstler [14x14. Young German Artists]*. Baden-Baden: Staatliche Kunsthalle Baden-Baden.

Richter, G., (1995). *The Daily Practice of Painting – Writings 1962- 1993*. London: Thames and Hudson, Anthony d'Offay Gallery.

Sontag, S., (2003). *Regarding the Pain of Others*. New York: Farrar, Straus and Giroux.

Storr, R., (2000). *Gerhard Richter – October 18, 1977*. New York: The Museum of Modern Art, New York.


**Image sources**

Fig. 1
http://www.tate.org.uk/images/cms/24749w_stonard_09.jpg

Fig. 2
http://www.gerhard-richter.com/art/paintings/photo_paintings/detail.php?7692

Fig. 3
http://www.gerhard-richter.com/art/paintings/photo_paintings/detail.php?7691

Fig. 4
http://www.baader-meinhof.com/wp-content/uploads/2011/10/EnsslinDeadM.jpg

Fig. 5
http://www.gerhard-richter.com/art/paintings/photo_paintings/detail.php?7690

Fig. 6
http://www.baader-meinhof.com/wp-content/uploads/2011/10/RichterMeinhofDeathSourceS.jpg

Fig. 7
http://www.gerhard-richter.com/art/paintings/photo_paintings/detail.php?7687

Fig. 8
http://www.gerhard-richter.com/art/paintings/photo_paintings/detail.php?7688

Fig. 9
http://www.gerhard-richter.com/art/paintings/photo_paintings/detail.php?768